MW01053389

Odin says,

"Jesus was a Coward!"

The Monotheist Subversion of Traditional Religious Thought

By
Michael William Denney

Introduction

Please allow me to address the title of this book. I know it will stimulate strong reactions. Let me be clear that I am aware at how incendiary the title is. I did not invent it for effect. This is actually what I heard in a dream while I believed I was conversing with the god Odin.

I cannot say whether or not I was actually speaking directly to Odin. I was, in fact, dreaming when this conversation took place. But, the content of the conversation was so shocking to me and felt so very real, that I woke up immediately afterward and remembered in detail what was said.

While this tends to persuade me personally that I was in fact conversing with Odin himself, I completely understand how the reader may simply conclude that I was conversing with my own subconscious while sleeping.

I am not opposed to this explanation nor am I opposed to accepting a possible simultaneous acceptance of both realities (especially when I consider the possible definitions of who and what Odin may or may not be).

I did not choose this title solely for shock value. However, it is my intention to convey to the reader the shock I received when I heard this phrase spoken to me in my dream.

The Setup

Without going into too much personal history, I feel I need to set the stage here a little bit.

For those who have followed my work and teachings, you already know some of my background and how I became interested in the pre-Christian religion of NorthWestern Europe.

To put it succinctly, after almost 20 years of studying, teaching and practicing shamanic spiritual disciplines from multiple animist and polytheist cultures, I became very interested in the indigenous animist and polytheist beliefs of my pre-Christian European ancestors.

I am of Scandinavian and Anglo-Saxon descent. So, I began studying the indigenous polytheist myths of my ancestors, more commonly known as the "Norse Myths."

In my childhood and early adulthood, I had intensely followed the protestant Christian religion of my parents. So understandably, the myth of the sacrifice of Jesus on the cross was an extremely powerful and prevalent influence on my spiritual thinking for much of my life.

After abandoning Christianity in my early twenties, I worked very hard to eradicate the whole idea of any higher power needing any kind of atonement sacrifice in order to commune with humans.

The whole idea that some omnipotent creator would go to the immense trouble of creating human beings in his "image" just to then summarily reject them as "evil" and consign them to an eternity of torment was abhorrent to me.

I rejected the entire notion that humans were in need of any kind of salvation. The whole idea of Jesus' sacrifice on the cross (ritual murder) in order to satisfy the anger of "God" against his own children was... well, I have no adequate words.

I'm sure you can understand my feelings even if you may not agree with them. So this was my mindset when I began to study the Norse Myths.

I was, therefore, intrigued when I began to study the story of Odin's "sacrifice" on the tree of life, which at first glance resembled Jesus' death on the cross.

For those who don't know the story of Odin's sacrifice, here is the mythological event in question where Odin sacrifices himself on the Tree of Life. Odin speaks:

I know that I hung on a windy tree
nine long nights,
wounded with a spear, sacrificed to Odin (the fury of
awareness),
myself to myself,
on that tree of which no man knows
from where its roots run.

No bread did they give me nor drinking horn,
downwards I peered;
I took up the Runes (mystical mysteries),
screaming I took them,
then I fell back from there.

At first glance, this myth seems to remarkably resemble the sacrifice of Jesus for absolving the sins of the world.

I had a personal aversion to the Jesus sacrificial myth, so I was having some difficulty with the sacrifice of Odin. As it turns out, as many moderners have done before me, I was projecting my post-Christianized world-view on a pre-Christian animist myth.

So, without further delay, allow me to now share with you the dream in question that completely obliterated my previous understanding of spiritual sacrifice.

The Dream

Often times when I want spiritual understanding to a deep question, during the early morning hours when I wake up from a deep sleep, I will allow myself to drift into a state of awareness where I am not awake, but I am still semi-conscious. In this "shamanic" dream state, I will state a question and wait for a response.

Sometimes nothing happens and I just drift off into normal sleep and dreams. But sometimes, I will be rewarded with a direct answer to my question. The answer may come in the form of a dream or in the form of a dialogue with a seemingly independent consciousness or sometimes I am aware that I engage in a dialogue with my own subconscious (whom I value as a valuable source of powerful information and revelation). This practice has proven very valuable to my spiritual training over the years.

So, one morning, while in this state, I realized that I was a little disturbed at the resemblance of the Odin sacrifice to the Jesus crucifixion. So, in my mind, I verbalized this question:

"Odin, what is the difference between Jesus' sacrifice on the cross for the forgiveness of sins and your sacrifice on the World Tree?"

To my absolute shock, I immediately heard this answer in a booming voice:

"Jesus was a COWARD!"

This was extremely shocking to me. It was also very frightening. I am still sensitive to the concept of blasphemy.

While I no longer believed in the Christian idea of sinfulness, I would certainly not have characterized the selfless act of willingly sacrificing oneself for the benefit of others as cowardly.

Even though I personally rejected the need for the crucifixion of Jesus, I would never, EVER have characterized it as an act of cowardice. Any such act, in my mind would definitely be one of extreme bravery and selflessness.

My previous years as a fundamentalist Christian had taught me that any being that questions the divinity of Christ was demonic. So, if the reader, upon reading this supposed response of Odin, had an immediate reaction that such a voice must have been the devil himself, be aware that such a possibility was not lost on me either.

This was no ordinary dream for me. I was still in a state of semi-consciousness and I briefly mused on the idea of opening my eyes and ending this conversation.

I decided that I was not willing to allow old fears to stop my inquiry. I chose to believe that I had the power to decide what I wanted to believe or not to believe and if this were some kind of demonic voice, I chose to believe that I had the power to investigate it and choose to accept or reject its validity.

I was not going to react from fear. So, I stayed with the dream state and continued to listen.

After a brief pause, as if aware of my internal decision to stay with the dream, the voice continued:

"When Jesus died on the cross, he took away man's most precious gift of the gods; the gift of self-determination.

Jesus GAVE away his salvation to a world that neither wanted it, appreciated it, understood it, nor earned it.

And look at what men have done with this supposed free gift of "forgiveness"...

NOTHING!

Jesus turned magnificent men into powerless sheep.

Odin's voice intensified and with increasing passion he continued…

I EARNED my enlightenment. I sacrificed myself to MYSELF.

GIVING enlightenment to one who has not worked for it is the gravest of insults. It says, that they cannot achieve it for themselves. No warrior ever acts this way toward another person.

Why would I demean and insult someone so badly to deny them the honor of earning for themselves the gift of Infinity?

A warrior gives all men ultimate respect. To die in the pursuit of self-awareness is the noblest of acts. If I thought someone was not capable of such an act, I would still allow them the honor of dying while trying to achieve it.

If I gave them my enlightenment, what use do they have of their own immortal divine spirit?

What a waste… What a colossal waste…

If Jesus or anyone else tried to GIVE me THEIR salvation that they earned, I would, like any true warrior, kill them on the spot for such an offense.

Unlike Jesus, I shared the example of my own sacrifice so that Men could replicate it for THEMSELVES so that they could equally share in the gift of Self-Evolution.

They, through their own efforts, can stand side by side with me, as warriors, not as pathetic sheep.

They need not worship me. They can worship themselves.

Anyone who endures such a self-sacrifice as I have, will never take it for granted. NEVER! It is impossible to do so.

But, look at men today. They respect NOTHING!

I was the first of men to sacrifice myself to myself and as a result, the eternal mysteries of existence revealed themselves to me.

The Runes (divine secrets) do not magically remove sins. They empower men to die to and transcend their self-imposed limitations.

The only path to true evolution is that of the warrior. Without the warrior spirit, men will fall. I am a warrior. Jesus is not. He is a coward and he teaches men to be cowards.

I will not condescend to mankind by attempting to change his mind. He has made his choice. He has chosen to abandon the path of the warrior, the path to his own self-transformation.

Man has chosen to give Jesus control over his eternal destiny. Jesus was a slave and a sheep and Man has chosen to follow Jesus' example.

I will respect man in whatever decision he makes regardless of how disgusting it may be to me.

For me there is only one sin; that is to deny oneself the realization of one's full potential."

Odin's words are pretty straight-forward. There is no need for me to examine or explain them. I will let them stand on their own merits and allow the reader to make his/her own conclusions about them.

Much more was said to me in that dream. Much of it was downloaded into my consciousness in heavily concentrated chunks that I am still absorbing, much like unzipping a large download file on your computer.

What is difficult for me to portray in my attempt to record this small portion of Odin's words spoken to me is even though he seemed quite angry and clearly passionate about his feelings, he also betrayed a stoic sadness beneath his anger.

I sensed that he felt that man's "conversion" to Christianity and subsequent rejection of traditional spiritual values was a profound tragedy for the cosmos.

"What a waste... What a colossal waste..."

In the midst of Odin's measured fury, (the name Odin comes from the Germanic word "Woden" which means "He who is consumed with the fury of awareness") he made it clear to me that his understanding of the warrior spiritual code would not allow him to mourn or lament.

I sensed that even though he wanted very much to seek to persuade men of the superiority of the warrior's path, his own warrior code, his own "Orlog," ("origin-law" that guides each person to their own specific destiny) prevented him from doing so.

As a true warrior, Odin was honor-bound to respect Man's choice. I felt that Odin had deliberately chosen to withdraw from the world stage in order to honor Man's choice of embracing Christianity.

My conclusion based on what I sensed from Odin is that the reason men stopped worshipping Odin was not because he had "lost" to Christianity. This wasn't a spiritual competition for him.

He was not a forlorn, rejected deity desperate for man's adulation who, without the worship of his followers, would fade into oblivion and out of memory.

Instead, he was a powerful, eternal, self-evolved being of total awareness that deliberately chose to step aside and allow humans to experience the inevitable effects of their choice.

Odin was a god of experience. Jesus on the other hand is a god of intellectual influence. Odin seemed to prefer practical experience over intellectual persuasion. As a warrior, Odin might say, "Well, they've made their own bed, now they have to lie in it."

I had the feeling that Odin had perhaps traveled to other dimensions to continue his spiritual learning. I also had the feeling that he had recently returned to our dimension. I like to think that perhaps we are entering a new phase of existence where people will once again seek to be consumed by the fire of the "Fury of Total Awareness" (Wod - en).

Well, you might ask, "If Odin had voluntarily retired from the world stage, how is it he spoke to you?"

Good question. I think simply because I sought him out and asked him a question.

Odin did not unilaterally force his opinion on me. Unlike the Judeo-Christian God who opens the heavens and parts the seas, strikes men blind and loudly blasts his message upon humans with his unsolicited advice, Odin's warrior code prevents him from unilaterally thrusting his message upon men.

But, apparently he is willing to share his message, if invited to do so.

So, there is still some hope for us after all...

A Lost "Warrior" Culture

There is something else, very unique and very powerful that I experienced while conversing with Odin that I would like to share with the reader.

Odin vibrated on a very intense level that I had not experienced in any other spiritual path before. It was a little overwhelming and disturbing.

I have since discovered that my discomfort was as a result of never having felt that kind of spiritual vibration before in my other studies. It was completely unique to my experience. It took a while to get used to it.

Over the years, while investigating different mystical practices from various cultures, I believe I have had personal experiences with various different deities and spiritual guides. Each cultural path has a specific vibrational "feel" to it.

I have found that the spiritual traditions of various cultures reflect the various Elements in nature.

The Four Elements and The Four Races

According to a Hopi myth, when human beings began spreading across the globe, the Great Spirit, gave each of the four races an Element to study and master.

The Africans were given Water. The East Asians were given Ether. The Native Americans were given Earth. Europeans were given the element of Fire.

I mention this Hopi myth because it has been my experience that the traditional spiritual paths of these various cultures do, in fact, reflect the Elements as presented in this myth. (I explain this more fully in my first book, "The Thunder Wizard Path.")

The deities within each cultural path, in my experience, tend to "feel" different from one another. For example, Chinese spirit guides tend to feel very "aloof."

They tend to be unassuming and tend to focus on practical guidance and proper protocol. If the student is not ready for a specific teaching, Taoist spirit guides tend just "disappear" until one is ready.

When studying Taoist spiritual practices (the indigenous spiritual path of China) with a Sifu (master), If a student shows a lack of maturity or patience or is disrespectful to the teacher or the teaching, the Chinese master will not get angry, he will simply quietly remove himself from the student or only interact with the student through one of his other students and not teach him directly any longer.

Or he may give the student some less advanced techniques and watch from a distance until the student has shown that he has matured enough to be able to handle the advanced teaching.

In other words, in order to make progress in Chinese spiritual practices, one must have subtlety, patience, self-control and discipline. This is congruous with the Ether element which cannot be mastered without subtlety, self-discipline and patience.

While studying African shamanic drumming, I found that, like Water, one must bring a joyful abandon to the art of drumming.

African teachers tend to toss you into the deep end and allow the student to become engulfed in the power of their world.

Traditional African drumming is very precise, but if one overthinks it, they can lose the rhythm. One must fully give themselves to the flow of the rhythm.

My African teachers had a joyfulness and non judgmental acceptance of everyone that can only be experienced to be understood. And, to me, they have taught me the essence of Water.

According to the Hopi myth, Europeans have been given the Element of Fire. My experience with Odin taught me about the true essence of the spiritual warrior and the spiritual element of Fire.

I am, ethnically, of Northern European descent. So, you would think that I would have a natural inclination toward the Fire element.

Yet, when I first started working with Woden (Odin) and Thunar (Thor), I was overwhelmed and a little frightened at the sheer power they exuded.

They also interacted with me in a completely unique way to which I was unaccustomed. The first thing that I noticed was a fierce love, commitment and loyalty. They also tended to be very expressive with their emotions.

This was in total contrast to my experience with Taoist spirit guides who focus on technique and rarely communicate their feelings or presence.

When I was first starting to contact the Teutonic deities in trance, I was transported to a wooden longhouse. On the walls were swords and shields. The longhouse was illuminated by blazing fires and torchlight.

The fires reflected off of the shields creating orange, dancing shadows on the wooden walls. Inside, it was very warm and comfortable.

There was dancing, drinking, music and shouting. I was surrounded by laughing, burly, bearded men who hugged me, slapped me on the back and welcomed me into their longhouse.

There were women in that ethereal longhouse too, but they seemed to hang back allowing me to be welcomed as a warrior by other warriors.

There was an exuberance and a joy that was contagious. It was a major party in there and I was immediately accepted as one of the locals.

But what struck me the most was the feeling of family, warmth and love. But it was a fierce love. A love of complete commitment and loyalty.

I had never felt that before... ever. The warmth of that place penetrated into my entire being.

You may remember my description of the Chinese method of dealing with students who make mistakes. The Chinese master does not scold, he just retreats and withholds knowledge.

Well, I learned something about unconditional love within the Fire element. When I unintentionally made a disparaging comment about Thor, he immediately became angry with me. In my spirit, I felt him shout,

" How dare you insult me! Never, EVER betray your family!"

And then, as quickly as it erupted, the anger disappeared and the warmth and love returned.

The intensity of Thor's anger was shocking to me. I began to feel attacked and hurt, but then I realized that his anger was not directed at me in the same way that humans express anger. There was no judgement or revenge.

After a lightning strike, the air feels cleaner and energized. Like the sudden flash of lightning that accompanied Thor's reproach, once he expressed his feelings, the anger dissipated and the unconditional love returned. In fact, it had never left. True love expresses itself without fear or remorse.

(I would find later that Thor also emanates a deep peace and boundless unconditional kindness. He is not always so fiery and explosive.)

Thor's honest expression of anger was the act of a totally committed, close friend who trusted me enough to honestly reflect how I was unintentionally hurting him. It was an act of vulnerability, love and commitment.

There was also a feeling of respect that comes with total honesty. There was no need for disingenuous, codependent, false kindness. These Fire people shared exactly what they felt and held nothing back.

And… wait a second…He called me "family." I had to think about that…

I wasn't just his devotee, I was a member of his family! In was in for life. There was nothing I could do to lose his love.

Unlike the Chinese master, who retreats and lets the student learn on his own, the Fire teachers stay with you in your mistakes and burn away the misunderstanding.

It took a long time for this to really sink in. I'll be honest, for a few hours after this encounter, I felt shameful and guilty until I realized that it was my choice to feel this way.

I had never experienced a family member who had an expression of healthy anger. This would take a little time to incorporate into my psyche.

What Thor taught me was that it was OK for me to feel hurt and angry and to express it. The Teutonic deities express their feelings openly and fearlessly. This is the element of Fire.

Fire is associated with the heart center, the center of love. Love means relationship. Love is intense. It is passionate. When one loves from the heart, it is given completely and totally.

When one commits, one does so passionately and without reserve and it is for life.

This is the element of Fire and it was my ethnic heritage.

Unfortunately, it is my experience that this understanding of the spiritual mastery of Fire has been lost to modern Western society.

We have become divorced from our hearts. We have retreated to the prison of our intellect.

Don't get me wrong. Intellect is important. Odin is a god of the evolved spiritual intellect. But, intellect without heart is empty and sterile.

"Intellect" is a latin word which translates as "to pick apart." This is exactly what the intellect does. It looks at our surroundings and picks things apart in order to identify them.

Intellect is important because it is essential for humans to be able separate and identify differences in order to function and survive in manifested reality.

But, when intellect is separated from its spiritual function, it becomes a tool with which we can easily become trapped within ourselves, cut off from the power of Spirit. We can become trapped in arbitrary, over intellectualized thinking that has little practical value in our lives.

For intellect to function at its highest vibration, it must be fueled with the Fire of the heart. It must be fueled by unconditional love.

This fusion of heart and mind was the legacy of the pre-Christian European people and it was lost to us when we allowed the sterile message of spiritual separation to divorce us from our ancestral spiritual heritage.

That heritage is the mastery of Fire and living from the heart. This is what the Teutonic deities offer the world.

When we abandoned our polytheist, animist heritage for the dualist, separation contained within monotheism, we separated our hearts from our minds.

And without this spiritual love, the fire of separation is literally destroying our world and our environment.

As the inheritors of the Element of Fire, we Westerners still spread fire across the world. Just because we have buried our ancestral teaching beneath the dualism of monotheism, does not stop the fire element from working through us. We still unconsciously spread fire everywhere we go.

But without the guidance of our ancestral spiritual teachings, that fire does not create, it destroys.

The fire we are spreading across the globe is not the inclusive fire of love but the destructive fire of entropy, the fire of separation. It is separating our hearts from our minds.

Once that entropic fire is released, it cannot be put back in its bottle.

The myth of the fires of Ragnarock that destroy the world is about the fires of entropy.

We are living in Raganrock now. And it is during Ragnarock that the warriors of Odin (self-awareness) arise to combat the fires of destructive entropy.

Spiritual warfare is not what we may think it to be.

The myth of Valhalla teaches that when someone dies in battle, they ascend to the "hall of the chosen" where Odin trains them to fight as a spiritual warrior.

To "die in battle" does not mean being killed in acts of physical violence. It means to live fearlessly from the heart without regret. It means to share your heart and soul with all those you encounter without holding back.

Those who live this way, have no attachments to this earthly life because they have lived completely. They have satiated their desires and shared their love with all they have encountered.

Since they have no regrets, they have no need to be reborn. They are free to ascend to spiritual heights after death and are free to help others in their "battle" to be free.

This is the call of the spiritual warrior. He condemns destruction, fear and cowardice where he finds it. He fights for the freedom of the heart and soul.

It is time for the spiritual warriors of awareness to arise.

If we are to save this world, we need that Fire of the heart and combine it with the spiritual intellect.

This is the message of the ancestral deities of Europe.

They are telling us to arise to our own awareness. They are telling us that we are running out of time...

Blood Sacrifice

Traditional blood sacrifice entails the ritual killing of an animal and offering the blood of said animal to a god or spirit in order receive favor or spiritual power.

While the sacrifice of Jesus is technically a blood offering, it differs from traditional blood sacrifices in some very significant ways.

To best understand these differences, we need to examine what traditional blood offerings were designed to do.

Traditional blood offerings were designed to achieve a dynamic balance between men and gods. The foundation for the understanding of the purpose of animal sacrifice rests upon understanding the traditional, polytheist, animistic world-view.

What is Animism?

The word "animism" comes from the Latin word 'animus' which means mind, soul, or intention.

Animism is a spiritual philosophy that believes that all things seen or unseen in manifested existence has a consciousness (animus) with which we humans can interact and communicate.

Animism is the original religion of all cultures on the planet. It is the original spiritual survival strategy of all humans. Every culture and spiritual path on the planet that has ever existed can trace its origins to a form of animism.

It is only in very recent centuries that human beings have abandoned their traditional animist belief systems.

Animism believes that the cosmos is a place of dynamic and sometimes violent or even seemingly chaotic activity.

This dynamic interaction of forces are not seen as random events but, rather, the expressions of various consciousnesses that sometimes are temporarily at odds with each other in the process of achieving a state of harmony and balance.

The main goal of animism is to help humans achieve a dynamic interdependent balance with the various forces in their environment.

Animist ritual is one main tool designed to help humans achieve a state of dynamic balance with a diverse and conscious cosmos that is always moving and changing.

Ritual sacrifice is an important tool of survival in animist religions.

Blood sacrifice is a ritualistic strategy for transforming life-force energy to become available to be utilized for the benefit of mankind.

Animists understand that life-force energy cannot be created, it can only be transformed. This transformation cannot happen without an exchange of energy. A "price" must be paid.

To pay this price, humans offer up to the gods something of value to themselves.

Traditional blood sacrifice offers up the life-force energy found in animal blood to the gods in exchange for whatever is needed.

The gods were believed to have the power to transform the raw life-force energy of the animal sacrifice into any form to be manifested on earthly plane.

For example, if a village needed rain for the planting season, the life-force of the sacrificed animal was given to the gods who were believed to be able to transform that energy into rain…a very simple and logical idea. Even a child can easily understand the dynamics of this interaction.

In human terms, if you want someone's help, you usually offer something of value in exchange for such help… OK, so you get the idea.

The reason why we see very little animal sacrifice in modern times is because our perception of the value of animals has changed considerably from that of our ancient ancestors.

The original reason that animals were sacrificed in polytheist and animist religions in ancient times hinged upon the human perception of the high value of animals.

In modern times, animal meat is plentiful. For our ancestors, eating meat was a delicacy. We moderners have easy access to meat 24 hours a day, 7 days a week, 365 days a year. Even the poorest of us in the developed world can easily afford eating copious amounts of animal flesh everyday if we choose to do so.

Conversely, in times past, unless one was wealthy, meat was not consumed on a daily basis. Animal protein would have been more routinely found in cheese, butter, milk or eggs. Meat only came from slaughtering an animal and promptly eating it thereafter.

But to kill an animal to eat was not done without the keen awareness of the loss of a valuable animal. Thus, animal sacrifice was a precious gift to the gods of humans' most valued possessions.

Sacrifice was no mere symbolic gesture for the average tribal person. Most animal sacrifices were accompanied by feasting of the animal by the whole village.

Not only did the individual sacrifice his valued animal to the gods, he also freely gave of its sanctified meat to the community at large where everyone could not only eat, but be blessed by the sanctified meat. Sacrifice was an act of generosity to all.

One practical reason why some modern polytheist cultures such as the Hindu, no longer practice animal sacrifice is because of the change in our perception of the value of livestock. There are other reasons as well, but in my opinion this shift in ideas is also because animals are more readily available than in ancient times.

So, for successful sacrifices today, modern animists must find other sources of life-force energy that is perceived to be more scarce and valuable than animal flesh.

Instead of animals, we can offer our own life-force energy to the gods in the form of spiritual vows. A typical modern Hindu vow, for example, may consist of intense fasts, lengthy meditations, mantra recitations, abstinence of sex, or other types of vows that can last from 40 days to one year or more.

In other words, nowadays, our own time and energy are far more valuable to us than the relatively easily acquired flesh of animals which can be found on every street corner.

Regardless of the source, spiritual sacrifice is the fee we give to the gods in exchange for their help in transforming energy into the form we desire.

Origin of The Word "Fee"

In ancient times, around 2,000 years ago, the Roman historian Tacitus observed that the Germanic tribes did not use money in their transactions. In fact, he states that they didn't even understand the concept of coin money. They traded mostly in cattle for all of their transactions.

So, when placating the gods, the Germanic tribes offered their most prized possessions up in sacrifice in exchange for the gods' help. That is why today we still use the ancient word for cattle to denote a sacrifice for a service or, as we call it today, a "fee."

("Fee" comes from the ancient Germanic word "Fehu" which meant "cattle.")

Traditional Blood Sacrifice vs Christian Sacrifice

So, to better understand the dynamics of the blood sacrifice of Jesus as presented in the New Testament, we need to take a closer look at how this sacrifice was supposed to achieve man's salvation in the Biblical narrative.

Traditional Animist Sacrifice:

The traditional blood sacrifice consisted of humans offering something of personal value to the gods in order to gain favor, spiritual power and accomplish a practical survival task.

Monotheist Sacrifice of Jesus:

The Sacrifice of Jesus is said to be the almighty Jehovah sacrificing his Son to Himself, in order to gain human adoration and simultaneously secure their "salvation" from the punishment of their sinful nature of which they were powerless to avoid.

So, do you see the discrepancy here?

The sacrifice of Jesus is backwards. Here we have the almighty supreme being Jehovah offering his own divine god-son (to himself) in order to do what? Gain favor from himself? Gain favor from men?

The whole mechanics of how the Jesus sacrifice accomplishes its goal is unclear. At the very least, this convoluted "sacrifice" reveals a gross fundamental misunderstanding of the whole purpose of traditional blood sacrifice.

Blood Colored Glasses

According to Christian dogma, the sacrifice of Jesus is necessary because God is unable to commune with mankind due to man's "sinfulness."

God is said to "hate" sin so much that when he looks at mankind, all God can see is man's sins. Since God hates sin, he therefore can't help but feel hatred toward mankind and want to destroy him in his anger.

Christian lore states that God is perfect and human beings are imperfect and tarnished by the stain of "sin." Therefore God requires a blood sacrifice in order to wash away the stain of human sinfulness.

Christian dogma states that Jehovah "blinds" himself to man's sinfulness by covering man's sin with the pure, sinless blood of his son Jesus. When Jesus sheds his blood on the cross, this blood is used by Jehovah to cover man's sins so that Jehovah won't see his sin, but only Jesus' perfection.

God's anger towards sin is pacified by the slaughter of his innocent son. Christians are taught that during a brief moment during the crucifixion where the sun darkens and the Earth shakes, God pours out all of his anger for every sin ever committed and every sin that will ever be committed onto his innocent son. Then his anger is appeased and God feels better and can forgive mankind. (Just think about that one for a while.)

By looking through blood colored glasses, Jehovah can look upon his own creation without being uncontrollably seized by anxiety and anger that apparently normally occurs when Jehovah is forced to view imperfection of any kind.

This sacrifice to atone for sins is supposedly an extension of the Old Testament Hebrew blood sacrifice where an animal "without blemish" is slaughtered for the forgiveness of unintentional sin.

This type of Hebrew sacrifice for the atonement of sins is recognized even by Jewish scholars as being in contrast with the type of sacrifices practiced by other traditional religions that utilized animal blood sacrifices for the purpose of gaining favor from the gods.

It is my belief that the Jewish "forgiveness" sacrifice was invented by the Jewish priesthood during the Babylonian captivity in 597 BCE and does not represent traditional tribal Hebrew polytheist sacrifices for blessings. (more on that later).

Missing The Mark

The original Hebrew word for sin is literally translated as "missing the mark."

So, even in traditional Hebrew understanding, sin does not imply evil actions worthy of punishment, it merely implies, innocent, unintentional imperfection of any kind.

If we analyze the symbolism in the word "sin," we see the human being compared to an archer who is intending to hit the target, but unintentionally misses the mark.

The idea is that with practice, the archer will eventually be able to hit the intended target. By extension, it is presumed that humans will also be able to hit their target of being a "righteous" person with continued practice.

This unintentional missing of the mark is in contrast to someone who is intentionally choosing to disobey or cause harm by their actions.

Therefore, according to Christians, the Almighty Creator of all life is incapable of accepting anything other than total perfection.

God is even unable to accept unintentional mistakes from his own creation, his own "children," who are trying to hit the mark, but make innocent mistakes as they learn and grow.

The obsessive inability to accept imperfection in one's own children would be seen as a psychological neurosis, if Jehovah were a human.

Yet, supposedly for Jehovah, the almighty, one and only creator, this perfectionistic inability to accept the imperfections of his own creation does not reveal a fundamental personality flaw, as it would, if found in a human. Instead, this inability to tolerate mistakes is supposed to underscore God's divine perfection.

From a psychological perspective Jehovah is clearly suffering from "narcissistic psuedo-perfectionism."

"Narcissists often are pseudo-perfectionists and require being the center of attention and create situations where they will receive attention. This attempt at being perfect is cohesive with the narcissist's grandiose self-image. If a perceived state of perfection isn't reached, it can lead to guilt, shame, anger or anxiety because he/she believes that he/she will lose the imagined love and admiration from other people if he or she is not perfect"

http://en.wikipedia.org/wiki/Perfectionism_(psychology)

Jehovah's demands of perfection on his creation is a projection of his own narcissistic demands of perfection upon himself about which he clearly feels deep insecurity.

Actually, as a narcissist, he doesn't really care if he is perfect or not. He just wants to be _seen_ as being perfect. And anything or anyone that gets in the way of him being perceived as such causes Jehovah great anger.

For God to be seen as even slightly imperfect makes him so angry that he is willing to permanently cast anyone who makes him look bad (by their own unintentional mistakes) into everlasting punishment.

Bear in mind, God doesn't just destroy these unwitting evil doers, he keeps them alive in eternal torment, ever aware of their mistakes.

For Christians, Hell is a place where humans are made painfully aware of exactly how they offended Jehovah...In Hell, they are made aware of every single solitary offense ever committed. They are forced to relive and be punished for each offense... FOREVER!

An interesting side note is that the word "Hell" was hijacked by Christians from the pre-Christian Germanic word "Hel."

Originally Hel was not a place of everlasting torment. It was the underworld where souls of the deceased who had not ascended to Valhalla (The Hall of the Chosen), would go to await rebirth. Hel was in many instances a place of feasting and merriment.

But since Hel was such an ingrained part of the traditional European mindset, Christians appropriated the same exact word and changed its traditional meaning to describe the Christian underworld of eternal punishment.

Original Sin

In Christian doctrine, man is said to be "born in sin." Which means his fundamental nature is sinful. It doesn't matter whether he chooses to sin or wishes to be "good." He cannot avoid being sinful in essence and in action.

Simply because his ancestors (Adam and Eve) made the choice to know the difference between good and evil (which for some unknown reason is a bad thing), all humans, subsequently are therefore stained with that "original sin" and are held accountable for it.

Perfectionism in Worship

This type of hyper-perfectionism in worship is unique to monotheism. Traditionally, the gods are NOT seen as constantly demanding perfection.

Their infrequent "anger" is more representative of natural states of imbalance where natural forces are seeking to achieve a state of equilibrium.

But, in monotheism, it is the Almighty who is at odds with himself. He has created these imperfect humans whom, he must punish. But, if he punishes them, then he is admitting to his own limited imperfection when he created them.

So, no matter what he does, if he forgives them or if he punishes them, he loses face and must admit to his own imperfection.

To resolve this dilemma, God performs a blood sacrifice to himself in an attempt to achieve equilibrium in himself.

But the harmony which should have resulted from his sacrifice of his son to himself doesn't quite take. He still must send the majority of his children (whom he forgave?) into hell for eternal punishment. "Many are called, but few are chosen."

Mankind is told they are born in sin, and Mankind is incapable of removing that sinfulness. Yet, God must hold man completely responsible for his unintentional sins.

Christians are told that even though they cannot choose to erase their own sin that they inherited, they are still given the gift of free will.

So, even though they can't help being sinners, they are still held accountable for their sins. They are told that they do not have the choice but to sin AND simultaneously, they are told they DO have free will and could have chosen not to sin but did so anyway.

Jesus, we are told, is the only human who had the purity of heart to resist the temptation to sin. But, he wasn't just any human, he was divine also. Since he was born of a Virgin (who was impregnated by God) and he escaped inheriting human sinful nature.

So, Jesus cheats a little, but for some reason, that is OK with Jehovah...

The game is rigged. There is no way to win.

Man's only hope of forgiveness is choose to "accept" the validity of Jesus' sacrifice for them. If man does not choose to believe in the sacrifice, it somehow loses its efficacy.

If one chooses not to believe in the Jesus story and accept him as his savior, then he has 'rejected' Jehovah's gift of forgiveness. Apparently, all sins can be forgiven except the one that disrespects Jehovah the most.

(Reminds me of a storeowner refusing to pay protection money to the mob)

But even the choice given to man is not really his to make because Christians are taught that no one can choose Jesus unless God allows him to do so.

Jesus' Reluctant Self-Sacrifice

Jehovah devises a plan to redeem his own perfect reputation and simultaneously "save" mankind from his punishment. God's plan is to volunteer his own son as a sacrifice to himself. Jesus does not volunteer. He is commanded to volunteer to be sacrificed by his Father.

The gospels are clear that Jesus did not want to be crucified. Later he "chooses" to obey his father, but the fact that it is not his own idea and he has serious doubts about sacrificing himself, sort of, in my opinion, invalidates the "selfless" aspect of it all.

Compare Jesus' hesitance to be sacrificed with the complete commitment of other deities in animist mythology who willingly sacrificed themselves for mankind:

Prometheus gave humans the gift of fire. He also taught men how to save the best portion of animal sacrifices so they could eat it afterward. For these gifts to man, Zeus had Prometheus bound to a mountain where his liver was eaten each day by an eagle. But even Prometheus is not punished eternally. He is eventually freed by Hercules.

So, too, was Odin's self-sacrifice on the Tree of Life completely voluntary without any hesitance whatsoever.

Compared with just these two traditional polytheist examples of deities sacrificing themselves for mankind, Jesus' reluctance to be sacrificed looks rather pathetic.

Sacrificial Flow of Energy

The flow of energy in a traditional sacrifice is upward. By this, I mean that spiritual energy (contained in the blood) is meant to flow upward to the higher powers who then transform this energy to then enable the descent of spiritual power down to earth which can be used by men to augment their admitted lack of power.

Jehovah's sacrifice of Jesus does not follow this law of spiritual energy dynamics. The Jesus sacrifice creates a confused, chaotic flow of energy.

Jehovah, in essence, steals the life force of his own son in order to empower himself to be able to forgive the limitations of his own creations who must then repay his "free gift of salvation" with perpetual gratitude and unwavering devotion.

Whereas the normal flow of life-force energy in traditional sacrifices is from Earth to Heaven and back down to Earth, the flow of the Jesus sacrifice is from Heaven to Jesus to Heaven to Earth to Heaven again???

The supposed mechanics of this sacrifice just doesn't follow any logic or common sense whether that be of a spiritual or practical nature.

From the perspective of a shaman (animist) who seeks to find a dynamic balance of energy, this sacrifice of Jesus would create a chaotic flow of life force energy that would result in further imbalance rather than a healing dynamic balance between men and gods.

And indeed in my own personal experience with Christianity, this is exactly what does happen within the heart and mind of the Christian worshipper.

The Origin of the Jesus Myth

In my opinion, the Jesus sacrifice does not work simply because, unlike the animist alternative, it is not a myth created to solve a practical human survival problem.

The Jesus myth is a product of the minds of Roman imperial politicians seeking a way to artificially impose the blood sacrifice mythology onto a political power play.

Historical Authenticity of Jesus

This book is not meant to be an exhaustive thesis on the historicity or lack thereof of the Biblical Jesus. I leave it to the reader to do their own due diligence on this subject. Besides, I have learned through experience that devout Christians are not

interested in objective evidence if such evidence
contradicts their beliefs.

Having been a zealously devout Christian myself in
my youth, I understand this mindset and also
accept the futility of any attempt to persuade
Christians to objectively examine any such
evidence.

Having said that, there is zero and I mean ZERO
objective, conclusive evidence of any kind that a
man named "Jesus of Nazareth" ever existed. In
fact, even the slightest attempt to objectively prove
the existence of Jesus during the years 0 - 33 CE
will reveal absolutely nothing. That is not my
opinion, that is merely a fact.

But, the lack of evidence does not disprove his
existence. So, I submit to you, what is to me, the
most convincing objective historical evidence that
the biblical Jesus of Nazareth did not ever exist.
That evidence is concerned with the supposed town
where Jesus is presumed to have grown up - the
Town of Nazareth.

The Problem of Nazareth

The evidence that definitively disproves the
authenticity of the gospels is the fact that the town
of Nazareth where Jesus supposedly spent his
childhood did not even exist in any form until at

least 100 years after his supposed death and resurrection.

Moreover, a town called Nazareth is nowhere to be found in the Hebrew Old Testament nor in any other historical document until long after Jesus' supposed death.

The city of Nazareth was a real city, but not during the supposed life of Jesus. Nazareth was founded sometime after 135 AD by a group of Nazarite (Jewish Ascetic) refugees.

The gospels were written sometime after the founding of Nazareth. The Nazarites were an ascetic Jewish sect closely affiliated with the Messianic movement and rebellion against Rome.

Since it was well known during the writing of the gospels that Jewish ascetics lived in Nazareth, this made this town a poetic setting for the writers of the gospels to present their fictional hero as having grown up there.

The archeological and historical facts concerning the founding of Nazareth makes the historical authenticity the Gospels simply impossible. The Gospels are fiction, pure and simple. Jesus is a fictional character.

If, as the fundamentalists would have us believe, the Christian Gospels are literal, accurate historical accounts, then the question of Nazareth poses a huge problem for the literal existence of Jesus.

The Gospels are absolutely and unmistakably incorrect when they assert that the city of Nazareth existed in 0 - 33 AD.

If that one fundamental aspect of the supposed historical account of Jesus is completely wrong, then how can any of it be trusted to be historically accurate?

We're not talking about an insignificant detail that we could easily overlook. We're talking about a fundamental pillar of the Jesus story that could not have happened AT ALL.

For me, every other very valid and persuasive arguments against the literal existence of Jesus (which are beyond counting) are unnecessary.

The New Testament Gospels are unmistakably clear; They are written about the life and ministry of a man who lived from 0-33 AD named "Jesus of Nazareth" who grew up in the town of Nazareth in Roman occupied Palestine.

The fact that this town did not exist until around the time that the gospels were first written down (100 + years after his death) makes it very clear to me that the Christian gospels are first century fiction most probably written by Romans, not Jews.

I have for some time now strongly suspected, as you probably have, that the Christian Gospels were the invention of the Roman imperial machine in order to use religion to control a very large and unruly empire.

Purpose of the Gospels

The original intent of the gospels seems to have been to pacify the very troublesome Jewish rebels who followed a revolutionary "messianic" form of Judaism.

The Romans very artfully studied the tenets of this messianic movement as well as the prophecies concerning the Jewish messiah recorded in the Torah.

Roman nobility, in an attempt to prevent the loss of precious time and resources militarily quelling a very stubborn religious rebellion, sought to create a fictional, pacifist Jewish messiah who could teach the rebellious Jews to "turn the other cheek" and "Give unto God what is God's and give unto Caesar what is Caesar's."

The verse about 'giving to Caesar' is an important verse because it specifically addresses one of the main flash points of the messianic Jewish rebellion.

The Jewish rebels were quite vociferous about NOT paying Roman taxes. To do so was considered blasphemous to Jewish extremists. It is no coincidence, therefore that Jesus tells his people to pay up.

The idea of obeying the Roman government was also a major theme in the New Testament epistles. In the 13th chapter of the Epistle to the Romans, Paul advises,

"Let every person be in subjection to the governing authorities (Roman elite). For there is no authority except from God and those which exist are established by God. Therefore he who resists (Roman) authority has opposed the ordinance of God; and they who have opposed will receive condemnation upon themselves. For rulers are not a cause of fear for good behavior, but for evil." ... "Wherefore it is necessary to be in subjection, not only because of wrath, but also for conscience' sake. For because of this you also pay taxes, for rulers are servants of God, devoting themselves to this very thing. Render to all what is due them: tax to whom tax is due; custom to whom custom; fear to whom fear; honor to whom honor. Owe nothing to anyone except to love one another."

The Jews of the day didn't buy into this new version of pacifist Judaism the way the Roman elite had hoped for but, coincidentally, Christianity started taking hold with other non-Jewish people within the Roman empire.

Eventually, the Roman general Constantine realized that he could use Christianity to great effect in his bid to become the next Roman emperor.

Constantine Becomes Emperor Through Christ

Constantine I, was Emperor of Rome from 306-337 AD.

Constantine secured his title of Caesar when he defeated the Roman Emperor Maxentius who was also a political rival claiming the title of Caesar. In the final battle against Maxentius in 312 AD, Constantine emerged victorious as Caesar of Rome.

"Conquer Through This"

Constantine was eager to consolidate his rule over Rome but there was another claimant to the throne named Maxentius whose military forces controlled much of the Italian peninsula.

Constantine, eager to defeat Maxentius and take the title of Caesar, was advised against attacking Maxentius by his generals, advisors and even his pagan soothsayers who claimed that sacrifices had indicated Constantine would lose to Maxentius' larger military forces.

Constantine ignored all of these warnings and proceeded to cross the Alps into northern Italy. From the spring of 312 to October of that same year, Constantine's forces advanced toward Rome defeating all of Maxentius' forces that he encountered.

According to various accounts, during his march toward Rome, Constantine had a vision of the symbol of the cross. He supposedly had a dream the next night wherein Christ told him to conquer by means of the sign of the cross.

On October 28th, 312, Maxentius' forces met Constantine's army at the Milvian bridge outside of Rome where Maxentius' forces were quickly defeated and Maxentius was killed during an attempted retreat.

Constantine rode into Rome that same day where he was hailed as a liberator by jubilant Roman citizens. He was declared Caesar of Rome shortly thereafter.

Constantine, The Opportunist

Constantine was, by all accounts, rather uneducated. Prior to his conversion he had been a pagan sun worshipper. Since he had been advised against attacking Maxentius by his own advisors, generals and pagan advisors, it is noteworthy to observe that Constantine continued his military campaign against Maxentius anyway.

It seems from his own account, that Constantine was not so religious that he wasn't above disobeying the gods.

A cynical person might conclude that Constantine was simply a headstrong, power hungry general who was not religious, but simply opportunistic in his allegiances.

We cannot say for certain whether or not Constantine's conversion to Christianity was a heartfelt experience or if it was simply an act of a determined politician seeking some kind of religious authority to his rule. ("Hey, if the sun god won't back me, maybe this Jesus fellow will.")

After securing his political dominion, Constantine legalized the Christian religion and began persecuting traditional pagan religions. He banned pagan sacrifice and sacked pagan temples and donated their riches to Christian churches.

While Christianity did not legally become the "official" religion of Rome until 380 under the rule of Theodosius, Constantine's support of Christianity effectively began the complete destruction of traditional animism in the Western world.

One Size Fits All

By the time of Constantine's rule, some two hundred years after the writing of the gospels, the Roman empire was long overdue for a state religion that would unify all the disparate cultures and religions within its borders.

Long before the advent of monotheism in Rome, the Roman empire would justify its conquest of other cultures with the propaganda that it was bringing the light of civilization to a dark and backward, primitive world.

But, this vast and growing empire of non-Romans created somewhat of a problem. As the Roman empire grew, more and more foreign religions were tolerated within the empire.

As Rome sought to gobble up the entire known world unto itself, it became harder and harder to unify such a diverse religious and cultural landscape.

As demonstrated with the messianic Jewish rebels, religion itself was a powerful tool for any would-be malcontents to motivate populations to rebel against Roman authority.

Since Rome saw herself as the "One True Civilization," it was only a matter of time before she invented a one-size-fits-all religion with which she could control all of her subjects.

Christianity, while initially invented to solve the rebel Jewish problem, was a ready made tool for increased control over the entire empire.

Enter would-be Roman emperor Constantine…

One can easily see the usefulness of a monotheist religion to create a monocultural empire. Better yet, why not a completely exclusive monotheist religion? Better yet, a religion that is so exclusive that anyone who rejects it will be eternally imprisoned and tortured for their blasphemy!

In recent years, more and more historical evidence has come forth that supports the idea concerning the Roman origins of monotheist Christianity.

For those wanting a more thorough historical examination of the Roman invention of Christianity, I direct you to the works of Joseph Atwell.

Another great resource for the mythological well upon which the Jesus myth is drawn is found in the first half of the film "Zeitgeist The Movie" (the second half of the movie is a bunch of conspiracy theory stuff that is not relevant to this subject).

Google either of those resources and you will find a plethora of readily available info on the subject of the mythological origins of the Jesus myth.

However, Christianity did not invent modern monotheism, it only built upon it.

In my personal opinion, monotheism is the single most destructive force ever unleashed upon the planet.

The "big three" religions of Christianity, Islam and Judaism are responsible for a monumental shift in human thinking that is unrivaled in the history of human existence.

During the previous 98,000 years of modern human existence before Christianity and perhaps even before that, humans evolved as animists.

Monotheism changed the course of human evolution and, as a result, changed the course of history not just for human civilization but for all life on planet Earth.

The Problem of Literalism

Institutionalized Christianity has been founded upon the concept of literalism. Christian source material is presented as literal, historical fact rather than religious symbolism.

This was a revolutionary approach to religion. Up until this time, all religions were known to be mythological, not literal. Humans in ancient times, actually placed much more authority in mythical wisdom as opposed to the literal knowledge of facts.

In modern times on the other hand, when we identify any belief system as being "mythological," it is often used as an argument against its religious validity. Our modern bias is to view myth as quaint, outdated, fantastical superstition.

Traditionally speaking, however, the mythological spiritual perspective did not decrease the devotion of believers. Rather, it increased it.

To better understand this, we can examine the holographic nature of mythical thinking among devout polytheists in traditional polytheism.

As I often do, I will use my Hindu cousins as an example being that Hinduism is the oldest and only remaining Indo-European religion that retains an unbroken connection into pre-history. As such, it is a very authoritative example of the traditional animistic polytheist mindset.

If you ask a Hindu if there is only one god, he will say, "Definitely." If you ask him in the same breath if there are many gods, he will respond, "Absolutely."

If you ask him if Ganesha is real, he will say, "Yes!" If you ask him if Ganesha is only a symbol, he will say, "Of course."

To the modern Western mind, this sounds like nebulous, confused nonsense. To a traditional, animist polytheist, this is the holographic understanding of a dynamic and conscious universe where light is both a particle and a wave.

In the holographic viewpoint, things can exist in multiple forms and in multiple dimensions simultaneously. To say that Ganesha is merely a symbol does not in any way diminish his actual and real existence in the mind of a Hindu.

To say that there is only one God while simultaneously saying that there are many gods only expands the possibilities of spiritual experience for the devotee.

This kind of thinking is very foreign to modern Westerners. This difficulty of Westerners to comprehend the polytheist holographic understanding of reality is directly attributable to the effect of the introduction of the dualist mindset of monotheist Christianity that aggressively sought to destroy the indigenous Indo-European polytheist world-view of pre-Christian Europeans.

A population that thinks in linear, dualist thought patterns is much easier to control than holographic, independent minded subjects who base their reality on personal experience rather than arbitrary intellectualized, dualist platitudes as is found in monotheist religion.

The main goal of the Roman elite who invented Christianity was to introduce this dualist mindset onto the empire so that they could more easily control and expand their rule.

This is why the modern Western world who has inherited and perfected the Roman model has become the dominant force in the world today. Dualism works if what you want is to destroy original, independent thinking.

The Polytheist Equivalent of Christ

The closest equivalent Hindu polytheist concept of Christ is that of an avatar of Vishnu.

The Hindu "trinity" is composed of Shiva, Vishnu and Brahma and which can loosely be compared respectively with the Christian concepts of Father, Son and Holy Spirit.

Two of the avatars of Vishnu include the well known deities of Krishna and Rama. (*In fact, Krishna devotees strongly resemble born again Christians in many respects. If you were to overhear them speak about their beloved deity and you were to* replace the word "Krishna" with "Jesus" you might never know the difference.)

One main difference between the avatars of Vishnu and the Christ-man Jesus is that the avatars of Vishnu are not, nor were they ever, thought to have been actual human beings. At least not in the literal sense that Jesus is depicted in the gospels.

The non-literal status of these avatars does not invalidate them in the minds of their followers. In fact, their mythological origin is wherein dwells their power. The mere fact that one cannot prove the physical existence of Krishna does not in any way detract from his experiential reality to his believers.

But, since the modern concept of Jesus has been built upon the idea that he was a literal, historical person makes his worship very tenuous. Because now, in order to be accepted, Jesus must be proven to have physically existed in linear time as we know it. He MUST be a real historical figure or else, the entire religion based on him comes crumbling down.

This literal interpretation of religion is a problem that no other religion before Christianity has ever had to struggle with simply because no other major religion ever claimed to be based on literal, historical fact. *(Judaism was a literalist religion that predated Christianity, but it was of little influence until Christianity hijacked it... But, more on that later...)*

Ancient people did not live their lives based on linear time. They had little use for such concepts. The seasons were cyclical, not linear. Life was cyclical. Every practical, survival strategy functioned within cycles of time. Linear time had little long term value to the average person.

Our ancestors lived in a mythological ever-present "now" that was experienced, enhanced and remembered through imagination and personal experience.

The gods and ancestors could be accessed and resurrected through myth and ritual. The gods lived in a mythical non-linear time that repeated itself through various natural cycles.

Jesus, on the other hand, was no longer on the cross. That was an event that had transpired in literal, linear time. He was no longer on earth with mortal humans. He was in heaven with his father. He was once human, but no longer. He was separate from his worshippers.

Linear Thinking is Unnatural

We humans have evolved over hundreds of thousands of years to experience time in a cyclical fashion. It is personally fulfilling for our minds to operate this way. The concept of death is more tolerable if we understand it is merely a transition in an endless cycle.

Literal, linear time is boring and frightening to our minds. Perhaps this is why monotheism stresses the finality of death. What better way to control a population, than through the fear of the finality of death.

According to linear, monotheist thinking, one only lives once within a linear timeline. The average person runs the very likely possibility that after death, there is only a horrific eternity of torture that NEVER experiences a transition. One is locked into a never ending timeline that never changes or transforms.

Come to think of it, when viewed in this fashion, the Christian Heaven sounds pretty boring too. Sitting around for an unchanging eternity on top of a cloud listening to angelic choirs singing the praises of Jehovah. Jeez, what a horribly boring existence! Which is worse, eternal punishment or eternal boredom?

This idea of a static eternity is not part of human experience. It has no positive effect on the human mind. It promotes a stagnant thought process. It dulls human awareness.

To function this way is not a sign of evolution. It is a sign that something is wrong with us, that we are out of harmony with ourselves.

The Desperate, Literalist Believer

If you say to a Hindu that Krishna was never a real person, he might say. "Of course he wasn't, he existed on a much purer plane than this earth we live on. He is far superior to a human like you and I."

As such, the faith of the Krishna devotee is unshakable no matter what arguments you may present to the contrary. He has personal experience with the holographic energy of Krishna and that is more real, satisfying and persuasive to him than any supposed historical evidence or lack thereof.

Yet, since the myth of Jesus was built upon the notion of his literal existence, Christianity has painted itself into a very difficult corner.

When I was a practicing Christian, I often heard Christians utter the following phrase:

"We worship a good God. I know my God is real. I know, absolutely **know** *in my heart of hearts my God is real and He loves me."*

I have never, EVER heard a practicing polytheist utter such a phrase. Polytheists do not struggle with such intense insecurity that they have to work so hard to convince themselves of the existence of their gods.

The intense, obsessive, repetitive assertions of the Christian reveal an intense insecurity within the mind of the Christian believer.

Having been a devout Christian myself for many years, I can attest from personal experience that I constantly struggled to reign in the confusion and doubt that plagued me as I tried to make the untenable contradictory elements of my faith make sense to my mind.

So, I understand completely why those Christians have to obsessively convince themselves that their God is real and that he is good. They must do so, because if they didn't, the internal reality of their experience of Christianity is constantly telling them that the vengeful Christian god is actually not very good at all and he does not feel real to them.

And without the mechanism of guilt and punishment built into Christianity, no one would believe it. Why would you? Who wants to trust their souls to such an angry, insecure, punishing god?

My point is that since Christianity founded itself upon the idea of literalness, it creates a very unstable base that is untenable in the human mind.

Simultaneously, the fact that Christianity is founded upon the presumption of the literal existence of Jesus, Moses, Noah etc... It has painted itself into a corner where the very validity of the religion itself invites scrutiny. And, of course, even the slightest attempt at any objective scrutiny as to the literal existence of such people will result in the determination that these people could not have ever existed.

Mythological religions, on the other hand, do not need to contend with this problem. The fact that Zeus, Jupiter, Odin, Thor, Krishna, Ganesha, Queztoqatl, etc... never actually existed in literal physical form is not a detriment to their respective religions but rather a selling point.

These are beings, entities, powers that transcend the limitation of time and literal existence. So, any attempt to objectively disprove their existence only opens up the human imagination to allow these beings to become more multifaceted than before.

The fact that these beings cannot have ever lived in linear time or limited 3-dimensional space only invites the mind to imagine them transcending human limitation. This is not only exciting, fulfilling and fun for our minds, but it enhances our ability to thrive in our 3 dimensional world.

The human mind has evolved the strategy of mythologizing our heroes in order to better interface with our environment. And this strategy works very well when we live in harmony with our external environment.

Once someone has had an experience with a mythological deity through their imagination, it doesn't matter what the exact nature of that deity is. Whether the deity is imaginary or literal can change on a daily basis and transform in order to meet the needs of the worshipper.

But a literal deity, becomes very hard to believe in when that form can never change. The human imagination gets bored of this stale, inflexibility.

And thus, we see the emergence of the tyrannical nature of "God the Father" who sends any doubters or unbelievers into eternal torment just for the sin of doubt.

Whereas, the voluntary and free fire of devotion is the fuel that drives the worshipper of the mythological deity.

Fear, guilt and shame become the only thing that keeps the devotee of the literal god in check. Without it, he would surely abandon the literal god for the sheer pleasure of the mythological beings that gladly seek ways to change in order to fulfill the needs of the human imagination.

This natural human aversion to the limitations of literalism sets the stage for the emergence of the "jealous" god Jehovah and the birth of modern monotheism.

Origins of Modern Monotheism

Monotheism as we know it today officially began in 597 BCE when the nation of Judea replaced their traditional polytheist religion with a monotheist nationalist religion.

Ironically, when first introduced to the nation of Judea, Jewish monotheism was a little known and peculiar religion that was very unique in the ancient world.

Despite what we have been taught in schools, temples, mosques and churches, monotheism was NOT the first religion practiced by humans. It is a complete aberration in human religious history and is a very recent invention.

And despite the Old Testament stories to the contrary, the Hebrew tribes before 597 BCE were actually polytheists not unlike every other polytheist culture in the world at that time.

It was only AFTER the Babylonian conquest in 597 BCE and subsequent captivity of the Jewish elite that we see the creation of a monotheist Jewish religion in the historical and archeological record.

Babylonian Exile

The Jewish Bible (Christian 'Old Testament') was written down during the Jewish Babylonian Exile which began in 597 BCE.

There is no scholarly dispute here. It is well known that the Jewish scriptures were written down at this time and brought back to Judea with the return of the Jewish captives after the fall of Babylon to the Persian king Cyrus the Great in 538 BCE.

According to Christian and Jewish religious mythology, the Hebrew people had a very long and ancient history with monotheism stretching all the way back to Abraham who was "called" by the one, true god Jehovah to return to the one, true religion.

This same biblical 'historical' version goes on to tell the story of the enslavement of the Hebrew tribes in Egypt, the deliverance of the Hebrews from bondage at the hand of the One True God Jehovah and the return of the Children of Israel into the land of Canaan where they "liberated" the holy land from the pagan Canaanites and founded the monotheist nation of Israel.

The Old Testament spends a lot of time chronicling the conquest of the idolatrous, polytheist

Canaanites and characterizing them as a foreign people the children of Israel.

This is the history we have all come to believe about the Jewish religion and monotheism.

However, the archeological and historical record tell a very different story about the origins of the Hebrew tribes.

According to the disciplines of linguistics, history and archeology, the Israelites are none other than the Canaanites themselves.

The Canaanites were a semitic people living in the land now known as Palestine who spoke and wrote a semitic language that evolved into the language known today as Hebrew.

Archeology has conclusively proven that the Hebrew language is a direct descendent of the Canaanite language. Existing writing from the Canaanite period has been conclusively determined to be an early form of Hebrew.

Even the Old Testament does not dispute this fact. In Isaiah 19:18 the Hebrew language is referred to as "the language of Canaan."

This scientific fact surrounding the ancestry of the Hebrew tribes is in direct opposition to the biblical account of the founding of Israel.

According to the Old Testament, after Abraham settled in Canaan, his descendants migrated into Egypt where they were subsequently taken into slavery where they suffered under the lash of Egyptian pharaohs, were forced to build pyramids, etc., until they were liberated by God through the miraculous hands of Moses.

We are led to believe that after their liberation from the Egyptians, the children of Israel wandered the desert of the Sinai peninsula for 40 years being tested by Jehovah until entering the promised land and conquering the pagan, idolatrous, Canaanite foreigners and thereafter founding the kingdom of Israel where the land of Canaan used to be.

However, according to objective scientific data, there was never any conquest of Canaan by invading Hebrew refugees from Egypt. There is also no archeological evidence whatsoever of the wandering Israelites in the deserts of Egypt.

According to the Bible, approximately 2.5 million Israelite men women and children wandered the Sinai Desert for 40 years before then being led into the promised land of Canaan by Joshua.

And yet, there is absolutely no archeological evidence of this biblical account of events... No evidence at all.

According to archeologists, it is literally quite impossible for 2.5 million people to have wandered through this area for 40 years without leaving ANY physical trace of their existence.

Furthermore, there is no historical or written evidence of there ever having been Israelite slaves living in Egypt as described in the Biblical account.

It is extremely unlikely that the biblical account of the enslavement of the entire nation of the twelve tribes of Israel could have occurred without any written or archeological evidence of their existence.

In fact, the only evidence of this entire version of Hebrew history is found only in the Jewish Old Testament which wasn't written down until during the Babylonian captivity of the Jewish elite in 597 BCE.

Polytheist Hebrews

According to archeological data uncovered in Israel, it is very clear that not only were the Hebrews directly descended from the polytheist Canaanites, but that prior to the Babylonian captivity, the Jews were also devout polytheists just like every other culture in the area at that time.

Archeological artifacts dating back to historical periods in the Old Testament where the Israelites were supposedly worshipping the "one true god" indicate that the Jews of this period worshipped many gods. Excavations of houses all over Judea during this time period reveal household altars dedicated to multiple gods containing idols and statues of various kinds.

According to the archeological record, the practice of polytheist worship in Judea comes to an abrupt halt at the time of the Babylonian exile when the Jewish elite were taken into captivity and the Jewish temple in Jerusalem was destroyed.

At the end of the exile period, there is a drastic change in the archeological record where all of the polytheist altars and idols disappear.

This indicates that the Jewish people make a sudden transition from polytheism to monotheism right after the return of the Jewish exiled elite from Babylon.

So, what happened? Why the sudden change from polytheism to monotheism?

Jehovah, the Protector of Judea

Jehovah was worshipped during the polytheist period. But it wasn't until after the return of the Jewish priesthood from Babylon that Jehovah was installed as the one true god of the Jewish people to the exclusion of all other gods.

Before the exile period, the temple in Jerusalem had an altar of fire to Jehovah who was believed to protect the Jewish state from foreign invasion.

As was the custom with many temples all over the world dedicated to various gods, Jehovah's flame in the temple was to be kept lit at all times. It was believed that as long as his flame was lit and regular sacrifices were given to him, that Jehovah would protect the borders of Judea from all invaders.

Well, when the Babylonians attacked and defeated the Jews, they sacked the temple of Jehovah, the sacred flame was put out and the temple was destroyed.

The symbolism here is obvious. By destroying the Temple of Jehovah and putting out the sacred flame, not only was the nation of Judea defeated but so was the god assigned to protect them.

It is believed by many scholars that what happened next during the exile in Babylon is what set the stage for the introduction of monotheism as we know it today.

The Babylonians did not take the entire nation of Judea captive, only the ruling elite. This would have included the priestly class. So, the Jewish priests had a problem; they had kept the sacred flame of Jehovah lit at all times as Jehovah had instructed them to do. They had also performed regular sacrifices to him. So, why did Jehovah abandon the Jews allowing them to be conquered and captured by the Babylonians?

The Jewish priests most likely reasoned that they must have offended Jehovah in some way. "But how?" they must have asked. What made Jehovah so angry that he abandoned his people?

(lightbulb moment)

"Jehovah must be a jealous god! He must have wanted exclusive devotion to himself only. We must have angered him by worshiping other gods and he must have abandoned us in his anger to punish us for our betrayal. If we return to Judea and abolish the worship of all other gods, Jehovah will love us again and protect our homeland from invasion."

As is already well known, the Jewish scriptures which form the basis of Christianity were written during this time when the priestly class and the ruling elite were in Babylon.

Like the Christian New Testament, the Jewish Old Testament is presented as being literal fact as opposed to mythological symbolism as was the case with all previous religions up to that time.

The main rallying point for the Old Testament is the literal interpretation of the story of Jehovah liberating the children of Israel from slavery in Egypt. Since this story has no objective basis in historical fact, where did this story come from? What was its purpose?

The actual history of the creation of the monotheist state of Judea probably went like something like this:

The Jewish ruling elite and the priestly class had just returned from being held in bondage for 70 years in Babylon.

Judea was most likely in a state of chaos. The ruling Jewish elite needed to strengthen their nation. They also needed something to explain their defeat at the hands of the Babylonians which would help them restore their power over the remaining common folk who had been without their rule for 70 years.

The elite needed a religious and political tool to unite the people under them while restoring military and political power to protect them internally and externally. In short, the defeated, Jews needed a new mythology to unite them. To satisfy these goals, the ruling elite brought with them an extremely powerful tool. A political tool combined with a religious tool.

It needed to be a strategic tool that would effectively crush any opponents by casting them as traitors and cowards. A modern political equivalent would be the Republican tactic of calling into question the patriotic loyalty of anyone in the USA who opposed the Iraq war by equating them as someone who "didn't support the troops." A tool that created a fevered nationalistic sentiment designed to dissuade anyone from any pesky critical thinking.

The returning Jewish elite brought with them a new, completely unique religion which focused solely on the worship of the protector god Jehovah to the exclusion of all other gods.

This new religion not only solved their immediate problems concerning reuniting the Jewish people, but it also cast the Israelites as unique among ALL other people in the world.

These downtrodden, defeated victims of imperial oppressors became the sole inheritors of the one true religion that worshipped the one true god that EVERY OTHER NATION in the world had abandoned.

They came home with the intent to erase their polytheist religious heritage which failed to protect them from conquest. They came home with a new religious system which we now call "monotheism."

It was a new religion based in fear. A new religion designed to eradicate instability by controlling everything and everyone.

By introducing a mythology where Jehovah is the savior of the Jewish people, the message was very clear; if you want to avoid being defeated and taken off into slavery again, you must worship Jehovah alone. Anyone who worships the old gods is a traitor to the security of Judea.

The greatest balm for one feeling the sting of ultimate inferiority is to recast oneself as ultimately superior to all others. This new Jewish religion served that purpose very well. In fact, it worked so well, that the Roman Empire hundreds of years later would appropriate it for similar purposes.

The equivalent of this kind of propaganda theme can be found in modern America where the fundamentalist Christian right-wing conservatives try to rewrite American history by proclaiming that the founding fathers were fundamentalist Christians who were seeking to create a purely Christian nation.

In every presidential election we hear the cries of right wing candidates who want to uphold the "Christian values of the founding fathers."

For anyone that has read any of the founding fathers in depth, the truth is far from this Christian mythology. The founding fathers wrote profusely on the dangers of fundamentalist Christianity and religion in general. But, please enjoy trying to tell that to the average follower of Fox News. But, once again, I digress...

Paranoia in the Ten Commandments

If you have read the ten commandments, you will notice that there are really only eight different commandments, not ten. The first three commandments are solely concerned with the exclusive worship of Jehovah.

When someone unnecessarily repeat themselves, it reveals an obsession. Why would Jehovah need to have three separate commandments regarding his exclusive worship?

This is because the ten commandments were written at a time when the Jewish elite were introducing a new style of worship while simultaneously seeking to eradicate an ancient, deeply entrenched, traditional, polytheist religion.

That is no easy task. People do not easily discard their ancestral religion. Most only do so under the threat of death. The penalty for disobeying the commandments of Jehovah often included death. Death is the commanded punishment in the Old Testament for the sin of idolatry.

The Jewish elite needed to strongly emphasize monotheism as the ONLY accepted form of worship to a population that had, for thousands of years, been devout polytheists.

As has been revealed in the archeological record, the average person in Judea had altars in their home to multiple gods and goddesses. The worship of the protector god Jehovah was done only by priests in Jerusalem. This is because Jehovah was the god of the state of Judea worshipped mainly by the ruling elite.

In order to keep control of the population, after the return of the exiled elite, the priestly class had to eradicate the practice of polytheist worship within the household. By replacing the household worship of polytheist gods with the state sanctioned worship of Jehovah, private worship automatically became a political unification tool. To worship Jehovah was to worship the state of Judea.

But worship of Jehovah in the home was thought to be far inferior to state run worship of him in the temple. The Old Testament is very clear in this regard; Only the priests were allowed in the temple, the "holy of holies" where if the priest made the slightest mistake in the ritual, he would instantly die at the hand of Jehovah.

This is a far cry from the average person, who only recently, could boldly and independently approach the gods in their own home. There was no need for perfection in worship. One only needed their devout intent.

Polytheism was the religion of the masses. This was a threat to governmental control. By creating a state religion exclusive to Jehovah, the priestly class could then have more control over the population.

To worship Jehovah was to worship the state of Judea. Jehovah WAS Judea.
By creating a religion which shared no commonalities with their polytheist neighbors, the Hebrew elite reduced any risk of unwanted assimilation of their intended subjects into other cultures or nations.

During the 70 year absence of the Jewish elite, it was very likely that the borders of Judea became very porous and insecure. There must have been a real threat of foreign influence, perhaps even the threat that Judea would be swallowed up by their neighbors and cease to be a separate culture.

One of the main themes of the Old Testament is Jehovah's anger over the betrayal of "his" people who worship the gods of their foreign neighbors.

There was no distinction between freedom of religion and treason against the state.

Polytheism by its very nature is an inclusive religious philosophy. It is also a religious world view that is empowering to the individual. In order to reduce the threat of personal liberty and foreign assimilation, polytheism had to be eradicated.

If the returning Jewish elite were seeking to reign in their scattering population, it served them to disempower the individual and make him subservient to the nation.

The most basic right of any people is the right to think for themselves. By controlling people's religious beliefs, the powers that be can control the whole population.

Why Egypt?
So, you may have already come the same conclusion as myself in that the story of Moses leading the twelve tribes out of Egypt is nothing more than an allegory of the returning Jewish elite escaping captivity in Babylon. The story of subduing the pagan Canaanites is clearly an allegory of the intent of the Jewish elite seeking to eradicate their own ancient Canaanite religious heritage which they feel failed them.

This entire new religious history had to have been written during the 70 years that the Jews were being held captive in Babylon. In order to avoid causing problems with their captors, in their new mythology they replaced their actual captors, Babylonians with the Egyptians.

Moses wasn't leading the children of Abraham out of Egypt into the new promised land. The Jewish elite were hoping to be freed from Babylonian captivity and return to their "Canaanite" homeland.

Elohim vs Jehovah

While Jehovah is the most well known name of God in the Old Testament, he has others. Among them is the name "Elohim."

Interestingly, however, the name Elohim does not translate as "God" but as "the gods" or "the powers."

The word "Elohim" is plural for "El" which simply means "power" or "god." Elohim is the exact same word used by the proto-Hebraic Caananite tribes to denote their entire polytheist pantheon. Their gods were simply referred to as "Elohim."

There is no confusion as to the meaning of the word. It absolutely refers to multiple deities, not just one.

Since we have already determined that the Hebrew tribes were directly descended from the Caananites, it is no great leap of deduction to logically assume that the Hebrew polytheist pantheon (before the Babylonian captivity) was also known as "Elohim."

The pre-Babylonian polytheist religion of the Hebrew tribes must have been a direct evolutionary continuation of the Caananite polytheist religion.

The creation myth in the book of Genesis most likely contained pre-captivity Canaanite mythical elements that were already probably well known in Hebrew polytheism.

The average Hebrew person was probably aware of the Elohim in the Hebrew creation myth. Most likely they had grown up hearing about the creation of the cosmos by the Elohim or "council of gods."

It would probably have been political suicide for the Jewish priests to completely remove the Elohim from their new creation myth and replace it with Jehovah.

Just as in the Christian conversion period in Europe, where existing polytheist traditions were incorporated into Christianity such as Christmas and Easter, the returning Jewish priests had to prevent alienating the Jewish masses from their new religion.

Removal of the term "Elohim" from their creation myth would most likely have been seen as blasphemous. It probably was just easier for them to reinterpret the meaning of the word Elohim to fit their new monotheist interpretation rather than remove it from their ancient mythology or replace it with the word "Jehovah."

This idea of plural deities remains throughout the early books of the Old Testament even in the monotheist version. In Genesis, the phrase "let us" is used repeatedly where the supposed singular deity talks to himself before accomplishing varying acts of creation. "Let us create man in our image,"… "Let us go down and confuse their language," "Man has become like one of us," etc,…

Ironically, it is this same plural word "Elohim" that is interchangeably used to denote both the almighty monotheist god of the Hebrews and also the false pagan gods that are to be avoided. "Thou shalt have no other gods (elohim) before me."

Both Christians and Jews have very elaborate and complicated justifications for the monotheist interpretation of the use of word Elohim in the Bible. But, the simple fact is that the writers of the Old Testament had the ability to clearly distinguish between the singular God and plural gods in their language. Just like in the European conversion to

Christianity, aspects of the original polytheist traditions simply refused to disappear.

Some Jewish scholars will tell you that God hid bchind the mask of multiple gods untll He revealed his true self to Moses in the burning bush and revealed his true name of Jehovah.

Since we have already deduced that the myth of Moses was an invention of the Jewish priests during the Babylonian captivity to reinforce the new monotheist religion, a more plausible explanation is that the burning bush was merely a dramatic symbol of the new monotheist god burning away the older polytheist religion.

This can easily become a very lengthy and complicated investigation. However, for me, the meaning of the word Elohim in Hebrew combined with the archaic meaning of elohim in the Caananite language is the undeniable smoking gun that proves that Jewish monotheism has its roots in Canaanite polytheism.

Jehovah, the God of Ego

Let us now examine the essence of the name Jehovah (I am that I am).

According to the Old Testament, Jehovah reveals himself to his prophet Moses as a burning bush who is called "I am that I am" or "Yaweh" i.e., "Jehovah.

Let us review just a bit of what Jehovah says to Moses in the book of Exodus, chapter 20:

"1 And God spake all these words, saying,

2 I am Jehovah thy God, who brought thee out of the land of Egypt, out of the house of bondage.

3 Thou shalt have no other gods before me.

4 Thou shalt not make unto thee a graven image, nor any likeness of any thing that is in heaven above, or that is in the earth beneath, or that is in the water under the earth.

5 Thou shalt not bow down thyself unto them, nor serve them, for I Jehovah thy God am a jealous God, visiting the iniquity of the fathers upon the children, upon the third and upon the fourth generation of them that hate me,

6 and showing lovingkindness unto thousands of them that love me and keep my commandments."

Notice how Jehovah keeps repeating all the different ways we are NOT supposed to worship other gods. This obsessive repetition reveals an insecurity ill fitting of an almighty being.

But, to the point at hand...What is interesting to me is the meaning of the name "Jehovah"...(I am that I am).

Why did he choose that particular name for himself? As the Almighty source of all existence, there are an infinite number of names that he could choose from. But, he chose to call himself "I am."

Why not, "I am all things and all things are I," or "I am thou?" or " I am thou and thou art I" or "I am the essence of all beings?"

Instead he chooses, "I am that I am."

Why does he choose a name that separates himself from all of his creation? Why not choose a name that inspires his creation to feel close to him. Why not reinforce a sense of kinship?

Why does the almighty Jehovah, who supposedly dwells in all places and times, take such personal offense at being seen in the heavens, the earth or under the sea?

Wouldn't he, if he is indeed the source of all things, automatically exist in all graven images and in all of these different locations? Wouldn't all of these different methods of worship, by definition, bring him glory?

Why does Jehovah get so jealous? (He even admits it!)

The reasonable conclusion is that he must not exist in any of those images and places he commands us not to worship. He must be the opposite of what he claims to be. He must not be infinite. He must be extremely limited. So limited, in fact, that the only place he can be found is within himself and in nothing and no one else.

Jehovah must the epitome of limitation.

And what about Jehovah's attitude when he meets Moses for the first time? Why does Jehovah choose to start his relationship with Moses in such an adversarial manner?

Here the creator of the Universe seeks out humans and supposedly reveals himself to the world in his full glory and shares his true name with those humans made in his holy image and his opening line to them is…

"I exist unto myself with no connection to anything or anyone else outside of me. Worship me and only me and if you don't worship me and only me, then you obviously hate me and I will curse you and your children for four generations. But, If you obey me and worship me, I will bless you."

How does this attitude convey anything other than the classic definition of psychopathic narcissism?

If these words were spoken by any human, he or she would immediately be categorized as a very dangerous, destructive, mentally ill person.

In fact, these are the same kinds of words spoken by mentally deranged psychopaths, Tyrants and serial killers. Why would we tolerate such an attitude from a deity?

In my opinion, Jehovah is nothing more than the most narcissistic aspect of the human ego. Worship of Jehovah is worship of one's own narcissism, nothing more.

And it makes perfect sense for the returning, defeated Jewish elite to channel such a narcissistic, impotent deity in light of the events leading up to their captivity.

The inventors of this new religion were the descendants of the politicians and priests who were recently shamed and embarrassed in front of their own subjects by having their country forcibly taken from them by powerful foreign invaders.

After their captivity, they were returning home to those same subjects who watched them (or presumably their parents) 70 years earlier being taken away in chains.

(I would be interested to know if the lengthy genealogies in the Old Testament corresponded with the family names of those returning to Judea claiming to be their new leaders. If, presumably after 70 years, the original elite who were taken into captivity were either dead or very old, it only makes sense that their descendants would return and seek to legitimize their family pedigree to establish their right of succession.)

These returning elite must have been terrified of losing their parents' previous claim to power and so they exhibited the classic psychological defense mechanism of projection.

They project their sense of shame and impotence upon their intended subjects. Fearing that their subjects will blame them for losing the country to the Babylonians, the returning Jewish elite, instead of facing their own shame and embarrassment, blame their own subjects for the fact that the ruling elite (their parents) were unable to protect their subjects from foreign invasion as they were expected to do.

The definition of "projection" in the psychological sense is:

"Projection is the misattribution of a person's undesired thoughts, feelings or impulses onto another person who does not have those

thoughts, feelings or impulses. Projection is used especially when the thoughts are considered unacceptable for the person to express, or they feel completely ill at ease with having them. Projection is often the result of a lack of insight and acknowledgement of one's own motivations and feelings."
(psychcentral.com)

Since Jehovah is symbolic of the human ego, the worship of Jehovah is useful to those who feel disempowered, who carry a deep sense of shame and self-hatred which characteristic of an already weakened ego.

Monotheist Jehovah is the perfect deity for those unwilling to address their ego-mania born out of impotence. Monotheism is also the perfect religion for those who wish to disempower those with a strong sense of identity who might pose a threat to their desired power over the masses.

The perfect way to unite all people is through a nationalist religion that disempowers the individual and elevates the priests and the politicians.

Such is the legacy of Jehovah:
He started out as the invention of a defeated ruling elite of a relatively small and little known country in the middle of the desert that was facing cultural extinction and assimilation by its neighbors, a feeble ruling elite trying desperately to assert their

uniqueness in a politically and culturally unstable environment.

By all accounts, this tiny, unnatural, illogical and awkward monotheist religion should have either died out or have faded into the background or have been overlooked by its more powerful and successful neighbors.

But, instead, slowly over time, this new belief of monotheism has grown to be the preferred method of religious, cultural and political control of a world-wide empire that increasingly dominates the globe now, 2600 years later.

Despite the good intention of the a small minority of well-meaning adherents of the 'big three' (Christianity, Islam and Judaism), the most heinous and destructive acts committed in the last 500-1000 years (colonialism, genocide, terrorism, slavery, ecological destruction, military aggression, etc.,) were all committed either directly or indirectly under the banner of monotheism.

Monotheism and the Empire Mindset

Monotheism can only work under certain conditions. But in those conditions, it thrives extremely well because it helps to justify illogical and unnaturally imposed philosophies that are not naturally unsustainable.

Conversely, animism and polytheism work well where people live in traditional hunter-gatherer conditions or in must live in direct harmony with their environmental resources.

Monotheism works extremely well when, the natural and logical methods of surviving the natural world have been subverted in order to facilitate the acquisition of inordinate amounts of natural resources in relation to the size of the population in question.

When any society seeks to acquire more natural resources than they can naturally replenish, it is necessary to impose an illogical mindset that uses warped reasoning to justify the untenable position which has been adopted by that society to take more resources than they can replace.

In such a context, a society must find ways to obtain more resources than they can find in their immediate surroundings. This scenario creates what I am referring to as the "Imperial Mindset."

It may sound like I am referring to modern Western society. Indeed we are living in a culture that utilizes an imperial mindset. The entire globe is currently living under an imperial mindset. We have been doing so increasingly and uninterruptedly since the Roman conquest period. But, this same imperial mindset actually has its roots in the ancient past.

The Romans did not invent the imperial mindset, but they perfected it. Even though the Roman empire itself has "fallen," the infrastructure of that empire, both mentally and externally has remained and been expanded upon since the "fall" of Rome.

I cannot definitively pinpoint the exact time and location that the imperial mindset first made its appearance on the world stage. Most likely it has erupted and faded away numerous times before it really took hold and began to flourish.

We can see archeological evidence of this mindset all around the world from pre-Columbian Americas, to ancient Egypt, Asia, and most certainly in Mesopotamia where it had its modern genesis.

Cataloging all of the instances of empires throughout history would require a much longer book. I am not an expert in those details and that is not the focus of this book. The reader is encouraged to research any ancient empire they wish in order to see how this mindset plays itself out.

Before Imperialism

Our natural survival strategy that we humans have effectively used throughout 98,000 of the past 100,000 years is that of interdependence within the natural world. The Imperial mindset completely disrupted that evolutionary strategy and radically changed the way humans now interact with our environment.

Before empires, human beings, in order to survive, had no choice but to live in direct harmony with their immediate environments. When someone today uses this kind of language ("living in harmony with Nature"), it sounds very new-agey and exotic.

But, for our ancient ancestors, living in harmony with Nature was simply the only method of survival available to them. It was also a very effective, practical and logical strategy.

If any group of people was not able to sustain themselves within their immediate environment, they either had to die or migrate somewhere else.

The Genesis of an Empire

In a nutshell, this is how an empire is born:

For explanation purposes, let's create a fictional, pre-imperial society that adopts the imperial mindset. How exactly does this happen and how does their mindset transform as a result?

Let's say that these people in our fictional example are hunter-gatherers who become subsistence farmers.

In order for them to survive, they need access to water, fertile land for growing food and sustaining their livestock. They most likely need access to wild game for hunting purposes.

If they experience extreme weather events such as drought, floods or extreme swings of temperature, these events have a very profound effect on their ability to survive.

So, their need to live in a dynamic balance with their natural environment is a very practical matter of survival.

To accommodate their practical needs, they practice a form of religion which reflects their real life experience and has served their ancestors for tens of thousands of years.

They practice an animist religion which recognizes the diversity of powers and influences that surround them. Their religion is an attempt on their part to understand and predict how to best live in accordance with the dynamic changes in nature.

They most likely are polytheists who seek to achieve a state of harmony with all the different aspects of nature.

They see natural forces like Sun, Moon, Thunder, Lightning, Day, Night, the shifting seasons, etc, as conscious entities with whom they can interact.

Indeed, they feel it necessary to establish a relationship with these forces in order to survive.

Their way of life, their means of survival are all integrated and all serve the same function. But, all of this is about to change, because these people are going to discover ways that seemingly take them out of this natural cycle.

This will change how they view themselves and their relationship to their environment. This change in perception is monumental and is a shift that divorces them from at least 100,000 years of human experience and evolution.

This fictional community of people discovers a method of acquiring a larger than necessary amount of natural resources.

For this example, let's say they discover how to grow large amounts of grain, much more grain than they have ever been able to grow in the past.

This is initially very good for them because the community now has a large reserve of grain to feed them through winter.

But, in order to safely store the grain, they construct grain silos wherein they store it.

Other surrounding communities hear of their neighbors' ample grain supplies, so they naturally become envious and they begin to steal grain for themselves.

So, in order to protect the grain from thieves, the community must recruit people to guard and protect the grain from theft.

But now, there are fewer farmers to work the fields because instead of farming, more and more of them are guarding the surplus grain.

Simultaneously, a result of their newfound prosperity, the community grows larger because there is more food available to sustain their growing population.

But, the community's need for more farmers, soldiers and land to sustain their growth is increasing exponentially.

The community begins to increase its armed forces and uses its army to conquer their surrounding neighbors. They enslave their neighbors and use their neighbors' lands for supplying their growing need for resources.

Meanwhile, the conquered neighbor population is taken into slavery to work their own fields for the benefit of their conquerors.

Within a relatively short amount of time, the once small subsistence farming community has now grown into a city-state wherein most of its elite citizens live densely packed within city walls for their protection against their resentful and fearful neighbors.

Inside their city walls, living in unnaturally close proximity to one another and their domesticated animals creates health problems from exposure to human and animal waste.

(*Many people may not be aware that the diseases brought to the New World by Europeans that ravaged the Native American population came into existence because of these exact conditions I am describing here. The creation of the imperial mindset actually brought these horrible diseases into existence.*

Small pox, tuberculosis, influenza and other infectious diseases came into existence as the result of humans domesticating wild animals and then living in unnaturally close proximity to them.

The influenza virus that mutates into a new strain every year and kills millions is the direct result of the mutation of a virus that is normally not communicable to humans. This virus starts out as a bird virus residing in domesticated fowl that is transmitted to domesticated pigs. Pig DNA is similar to human DNA. The once harmless bird virus mutates inside of pigs and then it becomes contagious to humans.

Every year, a new strain of fowl virus is transmitted to pigs wherein the virus mutates into a strain that is communicable to humans. Human farmers come into contact with the pigs and then spread the new version of the flu to other humans that spread it around the globe.

This process happens anew every year. That is why new flu vaccines are manufactured every year.

If humans never started domesticating fowl and pigs and didn't keep them caged near each other, these diseases would never have arisen at all.

As the reader may already know, most Native Americans died from these "civilized" diseases before ever seeing a European. These diseases spread across North America before the European colonization of the New World. Some estimates conclude that 95% of the Native American population died from European diseases during the conquest of the Americas.

Interestingly enough, when these diseases began killing Native populations, Native Americans believed that it was a result of evil spirits attacking them. As it happens, these diseases are the direct result of the imperial mindset created thousands of years earlier during the inception of the imperial mindset in Mesopotamia and later in Europe.

The hunter-gatherers of the New World were very literally killed by the imperial mindset. This mindset invaded North America in the form of these diseases before Europeans ever set foot on the New World. So, in a very real sense, those Native Americans were correct. The demons of imperialism killed them in advance of the European conquest of the Americas.

But once again, I digress... Back to our fictional example...)

As a result of previous developments, the city-state dwellers are no longer directly connected to the natural resources that sustain them. All survival needs such as food, clothing, timber, skins, etc., are brought to them from outside the city, often times from neighboring lands.

The ruling elite and upper class citizens are now completely disconnected from their immediate environment and no longer feel themselves dependent on their immediate surroundings.

They no longer feel a personal need to worship the traditional nature deities associated with farming. They no longer feel a personal connection to their ancestral animist religion that understood the concept of living responsibly within a limited eco-system.

The people outside of the city who are involved in the day to day tasks of harvesting food and resources from the natural environment are the conquered slaves and working classes who, although disenfranchised, are now part of this imperial system. The growing and harvesting they do now is not out of personal need for survival but by mandate of the ruling elite from within the city walls upon whom they are dependent for their survival.

So, as victims of circumstance, the laborers, too are divorced from the traditional understanding that one only takes what one needs for their immediate survival.

Instead of trusting the natural environment to provide for them, as was their ancestors' understanding. The common folk begin to see the natural environment as something to exploit. They begin to see the natural environment as something to conquer.

The growing population of citizens, slaves and workers continues to increase necessitating the acquisition of more resources.

You can predict how this imperial mindset begins to balloon out of proportion and creates a self-perpetuating cycle.

What used to be a society that identified with Nature who provided for them, they now identify as belonging to a nation or city state that provides for them.

They now feel a need to worship their country, their military, their government that provides for their needs through conquest and exploitation.

A Difficult Remedy

While this is a fictional example for the illustrative purposes of this book, it is almost identical to the events surrounding the birth of the Greek empire upon which Western society bases its "civilized" identity.

The Romans absorbed and built upon the Greek model. All of our "Western Civilization" classes in schools and universities across the world romantically look back to the Greeks for creating our Western civilized mindset.

The truth is that this "civilized" Greek mindset was very foreign to the vast majority of the indigenous European people until the middle ages. But, as this imperial mindset was adopted by the Romans and later the Christians, the conquered tribal Europeans were forced to forget their own animist history in order to function within the new European mindset.

This is why, today, in our Western educational system, we only study European history that begins after the so-called "dark ages" when Christianity was replacing the indigenous, animist mindset of Europe with the imperial mindset of the classical Greek and Roman empires.

Attempting To Erase Shame Through Rewriting of Ancestral History

Why do so many other cultures retain their historical identities that stretch back thousands of years and northern Europeans only retain an identity that goes back to medieval times?

Why do Europeans regardless of where they are from trace their genesis back to the Greeks and Mesopotamians?

Why do those of us descended from northern Europeans consider our pre-Christian ancestors as only "barbarians," "pagans" and "heathens?"

We are, like the returning Jews, full of shame and self-hatred.

As the Jews sought to forget their Canaanite heritage, we Westerners have chosen to rewrite our history to reflect only those elements of Europe that embraced the imperial mind.

The Jewish defeat at the hands of the Babylonians was so intolerable to the Jews that they had to completely distance themselves from their own descendants and create an entirely new history for themselves where the Canaanites were not their own ancestors but inferior, idolatrous, child eating, reprobates deserving of annihilation.

In what would be today a very non-politically correct historical account, the righteous followers of the one, true, God are commanded by Jehovah to slaughter thousands of indigenous Canaanite men, women and children and to steal the Canaanite's ancestral land from them.

There is not even any attempt to disguise this version of events. Jehovah goes so far as to command his followers repeatedly to slaughter entire populations including infants,

"Now go, attack the Amalekites and totally destroy everything that belongs to them. Do not spare them; put to death men and women, children and infants, cattle and sheep, camels and donkeys."
1st Samuel 15

This is not a unique instance in the Biblical narrative. This same procedure is carried out by the armies of Joshua in many different cities as the children of Israel conquer and commit genocide on the indigenous Canaanites.

Similarly, the European historical narrative as taught in our educational system reflects this same self-hatred. We don't even have classes called "European History." Our history classes are called "Western Civilization."

We don't even try to bother hiding the fact that we have no interest in the actual history of Europe. We are only interested in those aspects of history that involve us becoming part of the "civilized" world.

In historical accounts, Pre-Christian Europeans are most often referred to as the "barbarians" who sacked Rome. These barbarians are always referred to in the third person and viewed as antagonistic to modern Western civilized values.

We unconsciously identify with our Roman conquerors and view our ancestors through their eyes as they viewed these "primitives" who destroyed their glorious Rome.

It is only after these barbarians have converted to Roman Christianity and become completely civilized and absorbed into the imperial machine that we are encouraged to identify with them as our ancestors.

Just as the conquered Jewish elite could not tolerate the thought of being descended from Canaanites who were conquered by their neighbors for hundreds of years and felt the need to completely annihilate their very ancestral existence, so too, the Northern Europeans could not tolerate the memory of their ancient, tribal ancestors who were also continuously conquered and shamed by Romans for 400 years.

Stockholm Syndrome

As those who are abused, tend to adopt the identity of their abuser, the Western world is heir to this same psychological disease of shame and self-hatred.

There is a well-known stress induced psychological condition known "Stockholm syndrome" where hostages identify with their captors.

Stockholm Syndrome is a psychological phenomenon in which hostages express empathy and sympathy and have positive feelings toward their captors, sometimes to the point of defending and identifying with them...the bonding is the individual's response to trauma in becoming a victim. Identifying with the aggressor is one way that the ego defends itself. When a victim believes the same values as the aggressor, they cease to be a threat.
http://en.wikipedia.org/wiki/Stockholm_syndrome

Often times, conquered people after generations of conquest will adopt the cultural identities of their conquerors. This is exactly what took place after the "fall" of Rome by the Germanic "barbarians."

In my previous book, "Awakening Sleipnir" I go into great detail chronicling the abuse of the Gothic tribes at the hands of the Romans which precipitated their revolt which culminated in the "sacking" of Rome.

Prior to the fall of Rome, indigenous tribal Europeans suffered horribly at the hands of the Roman empire. For over 400 years, tribal Europeans from Germania, Gaul, Brittania and other locations were conquered, massacred, enslaved and harassed by the Romans.

After the fall of Rome, the Roman empire was occupied by the invading Germanic tribes who, only just recently had been foreign, conquered subjects of the Romans.

Just because the Germanic tribes had miraculously gone from slaves and subjects to conquerors did not erase from their psyches, the hundreds of years of abuse, slavery and servitude suffered at the hands of the Romans.

In a very short time, the victorious Germanic invaders of Italy and Spain abandoned their native language and religion and replaced it completely with that of Rome. This was a perfect example of the Stockholm Syndrome on a massive cultural scale.

In the case of the subsequent European conversion to Christianity, we not only adoptcd the idenlily of our Roman conquerors but have overcompensated in ways even the Romans would have been shocked to see.

This unconscious shame and self-hatred has then been projected onto all those whom we have conquered.

This is the true, if unconscious, purpose and legacy of dualist monotheism as practiced in the modern world.

This overcompensation toward destructiveness is not limited to language and culture. It is also deeply ingrained in our policies toward the natural environment.

One the main tactics of medieval Christian missionaries when seeking to convert indigenous, pagan, tribal Europeans was to seek to distance them from their ancestral worship of the Earth.

The indigenous European tribes identified so strongly with Nature worship that the missionaries aggressively sought to purge them of this mindset in order to more easily facilitate their conversion to Christianity.

The Christian missionaries taught that anything "earthly" was evil and worthy of destruction. The Pagan warrior code required that evil be destroyed.

As a result of their Christian conversion, formerly polytheist European tribes adopted into their psyches a deep fear and hatred towards the earth.

This unconscious fear and hatred toward the natural environment is played out in our modern energy policies to obtain and burn fossil fuels.

Even in light of scientifically PROVEN alternative sources of energy and alternative methods of farming and food production, we STILL choose to act in ways that are destructive to our own health and ultimate survival.

The only way, in my opinion, to reverse this trend is to become conscious of the psychological origins and motivations for promoting this destructive religious philosophy.

Through an honest attempt at self-awareness, perhaps we can begin to address our deep shame and self-hatred that we have inherited from our recent ancestors and hopefully reverse the damage we have inflicted upon ourselves and the planet upon which we live.

Am I Intolerant?

Practicing monotheists may want to accuse me of intolerance toward their chosen faith.

Certainly, many will find my condemnation of monotheist religions as being too extreme, especially those who have only experienced it superficially.

Maybe the reader has never been to church or only identifies as a Christian because their family did so. Maybe you went to mass a few times a year or only heard the stories of Jesus at Christmas and Easter.

What's wrong with the belief in a God of love and forgiveness?

I understand your point of view. But, I believe that when one investigates what Christianity really teaches, it is very difficult to see it as anything other than toxic.

I was recently having dinner with a friend of mine and his girlfriend. He and I had been friends in college and we lost touch with each other until recently. During the interim period, he became very involved in fundamentalist Christianity.

Before he tracked me down, he chose to leave the church for many of the same reasons I had done many years earlier.

He and I were passionately discussing the destructive aspects of Christianity at the table.

His girlfriend was listening to our conversation but since she had not had experience with fundamentalist Christianity to the extent we had, she was curious as to why he and I were so strongly opposed to it.

My friend commented, very astutely in my opinion, that because she had not become as deeply entrenched in the religion as he and I had done, she probably did not have any first-hand understanding of the toxic effects of Christianity on a person's psyche.

We mused that she understandably, probably saw Christianity like any other religion, just an innocent way for people to try and connect to something spiritual.

As such, she mused, "You guys should just be more tolerant of others' beliefs. They're doing the best they can."

She continued, "Y'know, for some people Christianity is just about receiving spiritual grace."

"Yes..." I replied, "But why should we need grace at all? Your question, while it sounds very reasonable and open minded, assumes that there is something inherently wrong with us that necessitates some kind of divine forgiveness. One only needs grace (forgiveness) if they have done something wrong....There is nothing wrong or sinful about being born a human."

Listen, I am not trying to argue that anyone who practices monotheism is a destructive, evil person. *(Although, I can't imagine someone choosing to continue practicing monotheism once they know the historical origins of the belief system.)*

It goes without saying that there are millions, perhaps billions of devout, practicing monotheists alive today who focus on the healing, constructive teachings in their respective faiths who accomplish nothing but good things in their lives and in the lives of others.

While these people may admit that there are some difficult and confusing aspects to their faith, they would say that these divine mysteries do not invalidate the beneficial spiritual truths contained within their religion.

They may argue that the majority of their beliefs, actions and religious source material are focused on virtues of love, tolerance and forgiveness.

This is very true. But, these noble teachings within monotheist religions, while desirable and arguably beneficial, are not unique to monotheism.

I can remember being taught in Church that the values of forgiveness and love taught by Jesus in the Sermon on the Mount were revolutionary. We were taught that before Christ, there was no such thing as unconditional love or forgiveness.

Preachers taught that forgiving your abusers, loving unconditionally and not judging others were concepts that Jesus had introduced to the world for the first time in human history.

But, the truth is that these concepts of brotherly love, tolerance, forgiveness etc… can be found in every major religion, including the ones that existed thousands of years before Christ was supposedly born.

The aspect of monotheism that IS unique to itself is the idea of exclusivity and intolerance of other faiths. It is a fact that the 'big three' monotheist faiths are founded upon vehement intolerance of ALL other religions.

Intolerance and exclusivity is what makes monotheism unique.

Those values within some monotheist teachings that promote love and healing are found in every other major religion and have no bearing on its uniqueness.

The teachings that promote exclusiveness are unique to monotheism. In short, what makes monotheism unique is that Jehovah hates all other religions and those that practice them.

To my Christian friends, I would ask this question:

How can you, in truth, be tolerant of other religions when you believe that the god you worship will eternally punish the adherents of those other religions in the afterlife?

It is truly possible for you to have unconditional acceptance of 'non-believers' while simultaneously being convinced that your God plans on destroying them?

While everyone chooses a religion because they feel it to be a superior path for them personally, most non-monotheists do not see other faiths as being invalid.

Monotheism, because it is based on the idea of literal truth, by definition sees all other belief systems as being "wrong" and all adherents to those wrong faiths as being "mistaken."

"Well," retorts the Christian, "You, Mr. Denney, believe that monotheists are mistaken in their beliefs. What makes you any different than me?"

This difference is that, in my universe, you can be completely mistaken and still have a blissful afterlife. In my universe, it is not a fatal sin to be mistaken. In your universe it is.

Not all Christians are fundamentalists. There are those Christians who take a less strict approach to their beliefs.

Many of these more moderate types may agree with me that there are parts of the Bible that are problematic. Some will even go so far as to accept those teachings in the Bible that reflect their personal values, while rejecting other parts with which they do not personally agree.

Some may find this be an open-minded compromise.

I disagree. I believe it is an approach based in co-dependence and ultimately harmful to the individual who takes this 'moderate' approach to monotheism.

I don't disagree in principle with the idea of taking the parts of one's religion that work for you and discarding those that don't work for you. But, that moderate approach only works inside a religion that is not based on literalism and exclusionism.

Monotheism is by definition, exclusive and fundamentalist in nature.

It is extremely difficult, if not impossible, to be a devout monotheist without either consciously or unconsciously incorporating the fundamental belief that your religion is the only literal truth.

The amount of mental gymnastics involved in simultaneously believing and disbelieving in the professed exclusivity of monotheism, reduces one's ability to think critically about what they believe.

Those Christians that do not believe in the literalness of their faith but still choose to identify as Christians are either hypocrites or do not fully understand the religion that they practice.

The entire Christian faith is founded upon the idea that Jesus saved humans from eternal punishment for their sins. It is impossible for someone to be a Christian without believing in eternal judgement for non-believers.

Christians are taught to "hate the sin but love the sinner." While this is arguably a flexible and open-minded attitude, the God they worship is incapable of adopting this mindset.

Once again, the discrepancy between God's perception and his devotees' is apparent. Imperfect, sinful people can separate people's actions from their essence. God apparently cannot do so.

Sounds to me like Jehovah should be worshipping his followers. They seem to know more about unconditional love than he does.

Listen, my Christian friend, it is impossible to believe in God's damnation of non-believers and simultaneously "accept" the validity of other religions.

"Well, Michael..." Asks the Christian, "What about your Norse, Hindu, Vedic and Taoist myths? They are not literally or historically accurate either. Will you dismiss them also?"

No. They were never meant to be interpreted as such. There is no need to adopt a fundamentalist viewpoint to follow mythological teaching. Nor is there any mandate to believe or disbelieve in them.

Therefore, the follower of mythological religion is free to believe or not believe at whatever level they choose to do so.

What Do We Do Now?

It is not my intention to suggest that everyone follow the same path as myself.

While I have chosen to integrate the pre-Christian world view of my animist ancestors into my existing spiritual practices, I do not know what your Orlog (personal destiny) has in store for you.

I do not wish to preach to the masses. I am not seeking to proselytize anyone into any particular religious path.

For those readers who do not have a spiritual path or who wish to investigate a path that follows a traditional animist understanding of our cosmos, there are many different paths available.

Some readers may not be religiously or spiritually inclined at all. That is fine by me also. (not that you need my approval)

My main goal in all of my work is to find ways to help us become conscious of the world view that has been downloaded into us all and gain control of how we choose to interface with our environment.

Our modern western society needs an awakening of consciousness. How that awakening specifically manifests is not as important to me as just the hope that it will manifest.

This is just my desperate and feeble attempt to do my part before I leave this particular life. I feel that an awareness of our how our present communal consciousness came to be has been revealed to me and I want to make sure that I have done everything in my power to share that shift in my awareness with as many people as are interested.

Once again, my words fail to express the breadth of my feelings. So, for now, I leave this collection of rantings with you.

Resources

For more information concerning Modern Teutonic Shamanism as I am teaching it, here are some links to my other teaching materials…

Web based material…
ThunderWizard.com

For books, instructional DVDs in Modern Teutonic Shamanism, go to the ThunderWizard.com page and scroll to the bottom.

Keep your eyes peeled for more books and instructional materials…

May the ancestors be with us all…

Michael William Denney
July 2014

Made in the USA
San Bernardino, CA
12 November 2017